POINTS OF VIEW

Should All Students Have to TAKE GYM CLASS?

By Amy B. Rogers

KidHaven PUBLISHING

Published in 2024 by
KidHaven Publishing, an Imprint of Greenhaven Publishing, LLC
2544 Clinton St.
Buffalo, NY 14224

Designer: Deanna Paternostro
Editor: Katie Kawa

Photo credits: Cover, p. 17 (top) Drazen Zigic/Shutterstock.com; p. 5 Robert Kneschke/Shutterstock.com; p. 7 (top left, top right) matimix/Shutterstock.com; p. 7 (bottom left) Sergey Novikov/Shutterstock.com; pp. 7 (bottom right), 9 (bottom), 13 wavebreakmedia/Shutterstock.com; p. 9 (top) vesna cvorovic/Shutterstock.com; p. 11 Fotokostic/Shutterstock.com; p. 15 Ground Picture/Shutterstock.com; p. 17 (bottom) Monkey Business Images/Shutterstock.com; p. 19 AxelRudi/Shutterstock.com; p. 21 (notepad) ESB Professional/Shutterstock.com; p. 21 (markers) Kucher Serhii/Shutterstock.com; p. 21 (photo frame) FARBAI/iStock/Thinkstock; p. 21 (inset, left) Africa Studio/Shutterstock.com; p. 21 (inset, right) StockImageFactory.com/Shutterstock.com.

Library of Congress Cataloging-in-Publication Data

Names: Rogers, Amy B., author.
Title: Should all students have to take gym class? / Amy B. Rogers.
Description: Buffalo, New York : KidHaven Publishing, [2024] | Series: Points of view | Includes bibliographical references and index.
Identifiers: LCCN 2023000532 | ISBN 9781534545250 (library binding) | ISBN 9781534545243 (paperback) | ISBN 9781534545267 (ebook)
Subjects: LCSH: Physical education and training–United States–Juvenile literature.
Classification: LCC GV223 .R63 2024 | DDC 796.071–dc23/eng/20230126
LC record available at https://lccn.loc.gov/2023000532

Printed in the United States of America

CPSIA compliance information: Batch #CSKH24: For further information contact Greenhaven Publishing LLC at 1-844-317-7404.

CONTENTS

Feelings and FACTS

Do you like gym class? It's the best part of the day for some students. They love playing sports, running around, and learning new games to play with their friends. Other students, though, don't enjoy those activities. Gym class isn't fun for them.

Some people believe that not every student needs to take gym class. Others believe gym class is important for keeping all students active and healthy. Before you choose which side you agree with, it's important to learn all the facts. That's the best way to form an educated, or informed, opinion.

Know the Facts!

According to the U.S. government, 77 percent of public schools in the United States require students to take some kind of gym class.

How you feel about gym class can **affect** whether you think it's an important part of your education, or learning. However, it's helpful to back up your feelings with facts.

What's PE?

When people talk about "gym class," they're often talking about the school subject known as **physical** education (sometimes called PE). Physical education classes teach students ways to stay active, fit, and healthy.

Not all physical education classes look the same. In some schools, students play **traditional** games like kickball. Other schools have walls for rock climbing, pools for swimming, or spaces for doing **yoga**! Schools might even offer dance classes instead of traditional gym classes. Some students have gym class every day, while others have it only once a week.

Know the Facts!

In California, students in grades 1 through 6 must have at least 100 minutes of PE class time each week. In New York, students in these same grades must get at least 120 minutes of PE each week.

Physical education often deals with learning many different ways to move your body so you can find an activity you like.

Staying Active, Staying HEALTHY

No matter what activity you're doing in class, the goal of any kind of physical education is to get you moving! This can help you stay healthy and grow stronger.

Experts have said it's good for young people between the ages of 6 and 17 to spend at least 1 hour each day being physically active. However, only 24 percent of children and young adults spend this much time moving their bodies. This is why many people believe all students need gym class. PE gives students time to be active and teaches them ways to keep moving when they're not in school.

Know the Facts!

Studies have shown that kids who take PE classes are more likely to be active outside of school and are more likely to stay active as adults.

After school, kids sometimes spend time on their phones or tablets or watching TV instead of moving their bodies. Gym class helps them stay active, and staying active helps them stay healthy. Physical activity helps **muscles** and bones grow stronger, and it can help keep the heart and other important body parts working as they should.

How Much MOVING?

Although most people agree that PE gets kids moving, some wonder about how much moving kids really do in gym class. One study found that students are only active for an average of 16 minutes in gym class. This has led some to wonder if gym class is worth taking time away from other classes for such a small amount of actual physical activity.

People have also argued that many students are more active outside of gym class. They believe students who play sports, take dance lessons, or do another kind of physical activity outside of school shouldn't have to take PE.

Know the Facts!

In 2020, 54 percent of students between the ages of 6 and 17 played an organized sport, according to the U.S. government.

At some schools, students can choose to play on a sports team instead of taking PE.

Mental Health MATTERS TOO!

People who support gym class for all students often argue that PE helps with more than just physical health. The sports and games kids are taught in gym class help them learn about teamwork, which is an important life skill.

In addition, physical activity can help students stay **mentally** healthy too. Movement can help reduce, or lower, feelings of **anxiety** and improve a person's mood. A 2019 study showed that kids who are physically active have a lower chance of having mental health disorders, or problems. Getting enough physical activity can also help kids sleep better.

Know the Facts!

Between 2016 and 2019, almost 10 percent of kids in the United States had been diagnosed with, or formally said to have, an anxiety disorder.

Some schools have started to teach yoga as part of PE. This activity has been shown to be good for mental and physical health.

Causing ANXIETY

Physical activity can help lessen feelings of anxiety in many people, but for some students, gym class can cause anxiety. If a student has trouble playing a certain sport or doing another activity in gym class, they might feel a lot of anxiety about it. It might even make them want to skip the class—or school altogether—so they don't have to do it.

Bullying sometimes happens in gym class too. Students who aren't athletic, or talented at playing sports, have reported being bullied during PE. Bullying might also make kids want to skip school.

Know the Facts!

A 2018 study showed that 34 percent of adults had memories of being **embarrassed** in gym class as kids.

Everyone has different skills, and that's a good thing! However, kids who don't have athletic skills might feel badly about themselves when they think about gym class. Some adults believe this problem could be fixed by letting kids show their skills in other classes, such as art or music classes, instead of gym class.

Building Better STUDENTS

Although feelings of anxiety surrounding gym class might make some kids want to skip school, studies have shown that physical activity can actually help keep kids in school. According to multiple groups of experts, getting the proper amount of physical activity can help students' school attendance, which means how often they're in school. Students who are physically active generally report lower rates of absenteeism, or staying home from school.

PE can also help kids perform, or do, better in class. Staying physically active helps kids pay attention and remember things more easily.

Know the Facts!

Studies have shown that physically active students tend to get better grades than students who aren't active.

People who believe all students need to take gym class believe it helps students in their other classes too.

What's More IMPORTANT?

Physical activity can help students in the classroom, but some people think it's not as important as directly preparing for important tests. Some school officials have cut gym classes altogether or have cut back on the number of hours kids have PE each week. They believe this time is better spent in the classroom, learning skills such as reading, writing, and math.

Some students spend less time in gym class because they need extra help in other school subjects. Almost 70 percent of U.S. public schools allow students to skip gym class for this reason.

Know the Facts!

According to a study done by the U.S. government, less than 4 percent of public schools require daily PE classes for students.

Some schools don't have the money to fund, or pay for, strong PE **programs**. School officials often believe the money they have is better spent on things for other classes, such as new books, computers, or tools for the science lab.

Your Point of VIEW

Some students don't take gym class or don't **participate** in PE in the same way as their classmates for health reasons. They might have an illness or a **disability** that makes it hard or impossible for them to do certain physical activities. Most people believe these students shouldn't have to take gym class or should be able to modify, or change, PE activities to fit their needs.

Now that you know the facts and have looked at arguments from both sides, do you think all students should have to take gym class?

Know the Facts!

In almost 40 percent of public schools, students can be kept out of gym class as a **punishment** for not getting work done in another class or for acting out in the classroom.

Should all students have to take gym class?

YES

- Gym class helps students stay active, which is good for their physical health.
- Gym class plays a part in helping students' mental health because physical activity can lower feelings of anxiety and improve a person's mood.
- Physical activity can help students remember what they've learned and pay better attention in class.
- Gym class can help build healthy habits that stay with people their whole life.

NO

- Many students are more active outside of gym class on sports teams or in other activities, and they shouldn't have to take PE.
- Gym class can cause anxiety in some students, especially those who are bullied during PE.
- Time spent in gym class isn't as important as time spent preparing for tests in other classes.
- Some students have illnesses or disabilities that make it hard or impossible for them to participate in gym class.

It's not always easy to form your own point of view, but it's important, especially about an issue that might affect you—like this one. Using a chart can help make things easier!

GLOSSARY

affect: To produce an effect on something.

anxiety: A mental condition marked by strong feelings of fear or nervousness about what might happen.

disability: A physical, mental, or learning condition that makes it hard or impossible for a person to do certain tasks or daily activities.

embarrassed: Filled with a feeling of foolishness.

expert: Someone who has a special skill or knowledge.

mental: Relating to the mind.

muscle: A part of the body that produces motion.

participate: To take part in.

physical: Relating to the body.

program: A set of classes or events related to a certain subject.

punishment: The act of making someone suffer for doing something wrong.

traditional: Following what's been done for a long time.

yoga: A kind of exercise that often involves stretches and deep breathing to help both the mind and body.

For More INFORMATION

WEBSITES

KidsHealth: "What If I Don't Like Sports?"
kidshealth.org/en/kids/no-sports.html
If you don't like playing sports in gym class or after school, this website offers some other ways to stay active.

Kids' Quest: Mobility
www.cdc.gov/ncbddd/kids/mobility.html
This U.S. government website helps kids understand certain disabilities that might make it hard for students to take part in gym class.

BOOKS

Audra, Janari. *Physical Health in Our World*. New York, NY: PowerKids Press, 2022.

Huddleston, Emma. *Taking Care of Your Body*. Lake Elmo, MN: Focus Readers, 2021.

Weakland, Mark. *This Is My School*. North Mankato, MN: Picture Window Books. 2019.

INDEX